RIGHT ROYAL

John Masefield

Illustrated by Cecil Aldin

Foreword by Rachel Hood
President of the Racehorse Owners' Association

Introduction by Miles Napier
Former Official Handicapper

MERLIN UNWIN BOOKS

This edition published by Merlin Unwin Books, 2013
First published by William Heinemann 1920

Text © the Estate of John Masefield 2013

Merlin Unwin Books Ltd
Palmers House, 7 Corve Street,
Ludlow, Shropshire, SY8 1DB

www.merlinunwin.co.uk

A CIP record of this book is available from the British Library.

Illustrated by Cecil Aldin
Designed by Merlin Unwin
Printed and bound by Melita Press

ISBN 978-1-906122-60-7

To my wife

FOREWORD

John Masefield's atmospheric poem is a thrilling and exciting rendition of every Owner's dream. We are swept along by the courage, beauty and fortitude of the thoroughbred – Man's best friend – and the tensions surrounding his rider's (over) confidence and wild enthusiasm for the challenge of the Chasers' Cup, a race based on the Grand National. Bookies, gamblers, crowds, swindlers, ladies, gentlemen and brave horses. It's all here and totally recognisable still, despite our changing times. The illustrations are evocative and inspiring.

The reality is, we all long to be riding Right Royal to triumph!

Rachel Hood, President of the Racehorse Owners' Association

———◄●►———

JOHN MASEFIELD
AND THE ENGLISH CHASERS' CUP

It was a dream that drove him to be mad. This theme is the driving force behind *Right Royal*, a powerful and dramatic poem which holds the reader in suspense until the very last verses.

Right Royal was first published in 1920. Two years later a new edition was brought out, illustrated by Cecil Aldin. The action of the poem takes place in the years immediately following the First World War. Charles Cothill, the central character in the story, has entered his steeplechaser Right Royal for the English Chasers' Cup at Compton Course. Although a fictitious race, the English Chasers' Cup has obvious parallels with the Grand National. It is run over four and a half miles and features formidable fences, including Dyers' Dyke, a thin disguise for Becher's Brook. The conditions of the race appear, like the Grand National, to be those of a handicap. Cothill makes reference to a withdrawn runner, "she's scratched. The rest are giving me a stone."

Right Royal has earned a reputation for being temperamental and ungenerous and his prospects in a race of this calibre are remote, to say the least. (Today no horse with so poor a racing record as Right Royal would be eligible to run in a race like the Grand National. At that time, however, the conditions for entry were far less stringent.) On the night before the race, Right Royal appears to Cothill in a dream declaring that he will win. "It's my day today – I shall not have another," he says. On entering the stable yard the following morning, Charles is astonished to find that this normally surly horse hurries up to give him an effusive greeting. The owner has a rush of blood to the head and backs himself to win with all he possesses.

Later that morning on the racecourse, Charles confesses his rash action to Emmy Crowthorne, his fiancée. Although she puts a brave face on the news, Emmy is clearly distressed. Not only has Charles's impetuous act placed their future in jeopardy; it has also revived memories of how her father's excessive gambling had reduced her family to bankruptcy.

Emmy is justified in her misgivings about Right Royal's chances. For this good-looking and well-bred colt had received a hard race as a two-year-old, filling him with a fear of crowds that did not decrease when he was switched to steeplechasing.

Sir Button Budd, Right Royal's breeder and former owner, belongs to a generation now virtually extinct. The owners of the big private studs of that time bred primarily to race the produce rather than sell them. They not infrequently employed private trainers. (For example, Charles Morton was private trainer to Jack Joel, a leading owner and breeder at that time.) Such owners often retained the services of a jockey who would ride only those horses which belonged to them.

John Harding, Right Royal's 'trainer' seems to bear no resemblance to the present-day members of the training profession. He is clearly not a licensed trainer, supported by fee-paying owners. Nor does he fit the description of a Permit Holder, who is licensed to train horses belonging to himself and his near relations. It is probable that Right Royal is trained under licence by Cothill and that Harding's role is that of head lad.

Although delighted by Right Royal's well-being, John is alarmed by reports of large sums of money being bet on Right Royal, who has achieved nothing in his career to justify the degree of market support. He is even more worried that the commission agent placing the bets (then often done on an owner's behalf) is doing so on orders from Cothill. He can foresee nothing but trouble:

> *"He'll finish ninth, he'll be forced to sell*
> *His horse, his stud and his home as well;*
> *He'll lose his lady, and all for this –*
> *A daft belief in that horse of his."*

The strain on Charles increases as the time of the race draws nearer. But Emmy gives him the much-needed moral support. She says "my darling, I feel so proud to see you followed by all the crowd."

When Charles canters down to the start his confidence increases. Right Royal is moving boldly and the fear of crowds which has dogged his career up until that time is gone. This is as well, for the atmosphere is electric.

> *There was the course, stand, rail and pen*
> *Peopled with seventy thousand men*

Seventy thousand spectators represents a small crowd, when set against the 155,000 who attended the Grand National of 2012. Jump racing did not then have the following that it does today. But this crowd, starved of sport during the war years, is determined to make up for lost time. The Grand National (and by inference the English Chasers' Cup), first officially contested in 1839, is a great British institution. There were then no Animal Rights campaigners to protest that the race was cruel.

A cracking pace ensues when the race is under way, the horses "smiting the earth with clods that scattered." Right Royal is jumping with boldness and enthusiasm and horse and rider are as one.

> *The beast's red spirit was one with his*
> *Emulous and in ecstasies.*

All is going well until they approach a hurdle. Many followers of racing will take exception to the appearance of hurdles in a steeplechase! But a writer of Masefield's standing should be allowed a degree of poetic licence.

Right Royal comes to grief at the hurdle, having been flurried at the take-off by a rival jockey. Cothill remounts but is faced with the seemingly impossible task of making up the thirty lengths between him and the rest of the field. However, he is encouraged by the memory of a horse winning after being left at the start and by the knowledge that the heavy going will slow the leading horses down.

The following passages are very moving. Although shaken by his fall, Right Royal recovers his momentum and is jumping boldly and cleanly. And the understanding between horse and man has increased by the reversal in their fortunes. Words pass between them through the reins. From Charles:

> *So you and I, Royal, before we give in*
> *Will spend blood and soul in our effort to win.*

And from Right Royal:

> *So I sulked like my sire, or shrank like my dam;*
> *Now I come to my Power, you will know what I am.*

By the second circuit the fast pace on heavy ground is beginning to tell on the leading horses. There are many fallers at the next fence. The line which states "They charged at the danger and the danger took toll," is intended for the race which Masefield is describing. But this equally fits the description of what happened in the Grand National of 1967. On that occasion, Foinavon avoided the mêlée of fallen horses to gain the honours of the race, giving his name to the fence at which the disaster occurred.

Charles's patient handling of Right Royal (he did not use his whip or hurry his mount) is rewarded and by the closing stages of the race Right Royal is back in contention.

Muriel Spark, author of a book on Masefield, has suggested that the finish of *Right Royal* might have anticipated the modern racecourse commentaries, now an established part of racing, but then very much in the future. Whether or not this is the case, it is impossible not to feel a thrill when reading Masefield's stirring account of the finish. The atmosphere is supercharged: the crowd from the grandstand shouting "Come now, Sir Lopez"; the tired horses, gamely summoning up a final effort; the tension of the riders; and the final climactic line of the whole race...

As to Charles' bookmaker having disappeared, in those days there were no Ring Inspectors to monitor and control the betting transactions on the course. But the story ends well in more ways than one.

Ninety years have gone by since *Right Royal* was written and racing has seen many changes. But there are many instances in the poem with which the modern race-goer will be familiar. The sense of anticipation as the crowds arrive at the meeting; the rich owner lounging in his smart new car with his beautiful wife; the calls of "I back the Field," from the bookmakers; the "creaking of leather" as two horses land over a fence simultaneously; and the electric atmosphere of the finish.

Where racing is concerned, poetry can often reach those parts of our senses that mere prose cannot. Any poem on racing must do three things. It must capture the atmosphere, convey the excitement of the race and expound the thrill of the finish. *Right Royal* does all three things and in creating the poem, Masefield has made an unrivalled contribution to equestrian literature.

By no stretch of the imagination could Masefield be described as a specialist writer on the horse. Yet *Right Royal* is revered by many racers and trainers. Paul Mellon, whose vast wealth from steel and banking enabled him to become a leading owner and breeder on both sides of the Atlantic, quoted from *Right Royal* when making the traditional winning owner's speech at the Gimcrack dinner, following the success of his colt Mill Reef in the valuable York race.

Madame Jean Couturie, a leading owner and breeder in France, so much admired the poem that she chose the name Right Royal for her brown colt by Owen Tudor out of Bastia. The new Right Royal not only became the champion of his year in Europe, but also went on to become a highly successful stallion. The late Dick Hern, many times champion trainer, was an aficionado of Masefield and could recite lengthy passages from *Right Royal*. The Poet Laureate became a friend of Sir Alfred Munnings, the President of the Royal Academy, a distinguished painter of racehorses and a keen supporter of racing.

There is ample evidence that *Right Royal* has been much admired amongst other equestrian writers. The late Joseph Allen, a leading publisher of equestrian books and the former owner of The Horseman's Bookshop (once located round the corner from Victoria, but now alas no more) included *Right Royal* in a bibliography compiled on behalf of the *Lonsdale Book of Steeplechasing*. Many anthologies have quoted Masefield's epic poem. Amongst these are *The Racing Man's Week-End Book*, by the late David Brock; *A Horseman's Companion*, by Dorian Williams; *Runners and Riders* by Sean Magee and *The Poetry of Horses* by Olwen Way. Roy Heron's biography of Cecil Aldin contains reproductions of Aldin's illustrations for *Right Royal*. And Lord (John) Oaksey quotes from *Right Royal* in his autobiography *Mince Pie for Starters*.

The late Dorian Williams has suggested that Masefield may have been "more the poet than the horseman." There may be a degree of truth in this, but Masefield's writing is today as relevant to racing as ever. No racing enthusiast can set foot on a racecourse without experiencing a degree of 'magic'. And Masefield is second to none in his ability to translate this magic into words.

Miles Napier, former Official Handicapper, July 2013

————◆◆————

Extract from Masefield's introduction to the 1923 US edition of *Right Royal*

'Then no one can fail to be moved by the extraordinary beauty of the English thoroughbred horse, his power, fire and mettle, and by his heroic energy and courage in the excitement of the race. Besides the beauty of horses, and their magnificence of energy, I was moved by the delight of speed, and by the realisation of the strange spiritual presences which are awakened to take part in human life in all moments of contest.'

RIGHT ROYAL

PART I

AN hour before the race they talked together,
A pair of lovers, in the mild March weather,
Charles Cothill and the golden lady, Em.

Beautiful England's hands had fashioned them.

He was from Sleins, that manor up the Lithe.
Riding the Downs had made his body blithe;
Stalwart he was, and springy, hardened, swift,
Able for perfect speed with perfect thrift,
Man to the core yet moving like a lad.
Dark honest eyes with merry gaze he had,
A fine firm mouth, and wind-tan on his skin.
He was to ride, and ready to begin.

He was to ride Right Royal, his own horse,
In the English 'Chasers' Cup on Compton Course.

Under the pale coat reaching to his spurs
One saw his colours, which were also hers,
Narrow alternate bars of blue and white,
Blue as the speedwell's eye and silver bright.

What with hard work and waiting for the race,
Trouble and strain were marked upon his face;
Men would have said that something worried him.

She was a golden lady, dainty, trim,
As like the love time as laburnum blossom.
Mirth, truth and goodness harboured in her bosom.
Pure colour and pure contour and pure grace
Made the sweet marvel of her singing face;
She was the very may-time that comes in
When hawthorns bud and nightingales begin.
To see her tread the red-tippt daisies white
In the green fields all golden with delight
Was to believe Queen Venus come again,
She was as dear as sunshine after rain;
Such loveliness this golden lady had.

All lovely things and pure things made her glad,
But most she loved the things her lover loved,
The windy Downlands where the kestrels roved,
The sea of grasses that the wind runs over
Where blundering beetles drunken from the clover
Stumble about the startled passer-by.
There on the great grass underneath the sky
She loved to ride with him for hours on hours,
Smelling the seasoned grass and those small flowers,
Milkworts and thymes, that grow upon the Downs.
There from a chalk edge they would see the towns:
Smoke above trees, by day, or spires of churches
Gleaming with swinging wind-cocks on their perches.
Or windows flashing in the light, or trains
Burrowing below white smoke across the plains.
By night, the darkness of the valley set
With scattered lights to where the ridges met
And three great glares making the heaven dun,
Oxford and Wallingford and Abingdon.

"Dear, in an hour," said Charles, "the race begins.
Before I start I must confess my sins.
For I have sinned, and now it troubles me."

"I saw that you were sad," said Emily.

"Before I speak," said Charles, "I must premise.
You were not here to help me to be wise,
And something happened, difficult to tell.
Even if I sinned, I feel I acted well,
From inspiration, mad as that may seem.
Just at the grey of dawn I had a dream.

It was the strangest dream I ever had.
It was the dream that drove me to be mad.

I dreamed I stood upon the race-course here,
Watching a blinding rainstorm blowing clear,
And as it blew away, I said aloud,
'That rain will make soft going on the ploughed.'
And instantly I saw the whole great course,
The grass, the brooks, the fences toppt with gorse,

Gleam in the sun; and all the ploughland shone
Blue, like a marsh, though now the rain had gone.
And in my dream I said, 'That plough will be
Terrible work for some, but not for me.
Not for Right Royal.'

                  And a voice said, 'No,
Not for Right Royal.'

                  And I looked, and, lo!
There was Right Royal, speaking, at my side.
The horse's very self, and yet his hide
Was like, what shall I say? like pearl on fire,
A white soft glow of burning that did twire
Like soft white-heat with every breath he drew.
A glow, with utter brightness running through;
Most splendid, though I cannot make you see.

His great crest glittered as he looked at me
Criniered with spitting sparks; he stamped the ground
All cock and fire, trembling like a hound,
And glad of me, and eager to declare
His horse's mind.

                  And I was made aware
That, being a horse, his mind could only say
Few things to me. He said, 'It is my day,
My day, today; I shall not have another.'

And as he spoke he seemed a younger brother,
Most near, and yet a horse, and then he grinned
And tossed his crest and crinier to the wind,
And looked down to the Water with an eye
All fire of soul to gallop dreadfully.

All this was strange, but then a stranger thing
Came afterwards. I woke all shivering
With wonder and excitement, yet with dread
Lest the dream meant that Royal should be dead,
Lest he had died and come to tell me so.
I hurried out; no need to hurry, though;
There he was shining like a morning star.
Now hark. You know how cold his manners are,
Never a whinny for his dearest friend.
Today he heard me at the courtyard end,
He left his breakfast with a shattering call,
A View Halloo, and, swinging in his stall,
Ran up to nuzzle me with signs of joy.
It staggered Harding and the stable-boy,
And Harding said, 'What's come to him today?
He must have had a dream he beat the bay.'

Now that was strange; and, what was stranger, this.
I know he tried to say those words of his,
'It is my day; and Harding turned to me:
'It is his day today, that's plain to see.'
Right Royal nuzzled at me as he spoke.
That staggered me. I felt that I should choke.
It came so pat upon my unsaid thought,
I asked him what he meant.
                              He answered, 'Naught.
It only came into my head to say.
But there it is. Today's Right Royal's day.'

That was the dream. I cannot put the glory
With which it filled my being in a story.
No one can tell a dream.
                              Now to confess.
The dream made daily life a nothingness,
Merely a mould which white-hot beauty fills,
Pure from some source of passionate joys and skills.
And being flooded with my vision thus,
Certain of winning, puffed and glorious,
Walking upon this earth-top like a king,
My judgment went. I did a foolish thing;
I backed myself to win with all I had.

Now that it's done I see that it was mad,
But still, I had to do it, feeling so.
That is the full confession; now you know."

SHE. The thing is done, and being done, must be.
You cannot hedge. Would you had talked with me
Before you plunged. But there, the thing is done.

HE. Do not exaggerate the risks I run.
Right Royal was a bad horse in the past,
A rogue, a cur, but he is cured at last;
For I was right, his former owner wrong,
He is a game good 'chaser, going strong.
He and my lucky star may pull me through.

SHE. O grant they may; but think what's racing you,
Think for a moment what his chances are
Against Sir Lopez, Soyland, Kubbadar.

HE. You said you thought Sir Lopez past his best.
I do, myself.

SHE.   But there are all the rest.
Peterkinooks, Red Ember, Counter Vair,
And then Grey Glory and the Irish mare.

HE. She's scratched. The rest are giving me a stone.
Unless the field hides something quite unknown
I stand a chance. The going favours me.
The ploughland will be bogland certainly,
After this rain. If Royal keeps his nerve,
If no one cannons me at jump or swerve,
I stand a chance. And though I dread to fail,
This passionate dream that drives me like a sail
Runs in my blood, and cries, that I shall win.

SHE. Please Heaven you may; but now (for me) begin
Again the horrors that I cannot tell,
Horrors that made my childhood such a hell,
Watching my Father near the gambler's grave
Step after step, yet impotent to save.

You do not know, I never let you know,
The horror of those days of long ago
When Father raced to ruin. Every night
After my Mother took away the light,
For weeks before each meeting, I would see
Horrible horses looking down on me,
Laughing and saying, "We shall beat your Father."
Then when the meetings came I used to gather
Close up to Mother, and we used to pray,
"O God, for Christ's sake, let him win today."
And then we had to watch for his return,
Craning our necks to see if we could learn,
Before he entered, what the week had been.

Now I shall look on such another scene
Of waiting on the race-chance. For today,
Just as I did with Father, I shall say,
"Yes, he'll be beaten by a head, or break
A stirrup leather at the wall, or take
The brook too slow, and, then, all will be lost."

Daily, in mind, I saw the Winning Post,
The Straight, and all the horses' glimmering forms
Rushing between the railings' yelling swarms,
My Father's colours leading. Every day,
Closing my eyes, I saw them die away,
In the last strides, and lose, lose by a neck,
Lose by an inch, but lose, and bring the wreck
A day's march nearer. Now begins again
The agony of waiting for the pain,
The agony of watching ruin come
Out of man's dreams to overwhelm a home.

Go now, my dear. Before the race is due
We'll meet again, and then I'll speak with you.

IN a race-course box behind the Stand
Right Royal shone from a strapper's hand.
A big dark bay with a restless tread,
Fetlock deep in a wheat-straw bed;
A noble horse of a nervy blood,
By O Mon Roi out of Rectitude.
Something quick in his eye and ear
Gave a hint that he might be queer.
In front, he was all 'to a horseman's mind;
Some thought him a trifle light behind.
By two good points might his rank be known,
A beautiful head and a Jumping Bone.

He had been the hope of Sir Button Budd,
Who bred him there at the Fletchings stud,
But the Fletchings jockey had flogged him cold
In a narrow thing as a two-year-old.
After that, with his sulks and swerves,
Dread of the crowd and fits of nerves,
Like a wastrel bee who makes no honey,
He had hardly earned his entry money.

11

Liking him still, though he failed at racing,
Sir Button trained him for steeple-chasing.
He jumped like a stag, but his heart was cowed;
Nothing would make him face the crowd.
When he reached the Straight where the crowds began
He would make no effort for any man.

Sir Button sold him, Charles Cothill bought him,
Rode him to hounds and soothed and taught him.
After two years' care Charles felt assured
That his horse's broken heart was cured,
And the jangled nerves in tune again.

And now, as proud as a King of Spain,
He moved in his box with a restless tread,
His eyes like sparks in his lovely head,
Ready to run between the roar
Of the stands that face the Straight once more;
Ready to race, though blown, though beat,

As long as his will could lift his feet;
Ready to burst his heart to pass
Each gasping horse in that street of grass.

John Harding said to his stable-boy:
"Would looks were deeds, for he looks a joy.
He's come on well in the last ten days."
The horse looked up at the note of praise;
He fixed his eye upon Harding's eye,
Then he put all thought of Harding by,
Then his ears went back and he clipped all clean
The manger's well where his oats had been.

John Harding walked to the stable-yard,
His brow was worried with thinking hard.
He thought, "His sire was a Derby winner,
His legs are steel, and he loves his dinner,
And yet of old, when they made him race,
He sulked or funked like a real disgrace;
Now for man or horse, I say, it's plain,
That what once he's been, he'll be again.

For all his looks, I'll take my oath
That horse is a cur, and slack as sloth.

He'll funk at a great big field like this,
And the lad won't cure that sloth of his.
He stands no chance, and yet Bungay says
He's been backed all morning a hundred ways.

He was twenty to one last night, by Heaven:
Twenty to one, and now he's seven.

Well, one of these fools whom fortune loves
Has made up his mind to go for the gloves;
But here's Dick Cappell to bring me news."

Dick Cappell came from a London Mews,
His fleshless face was a stretcht skin sheath
For the narrow pear of the skull beneath.
He had cold blue eyes, and a mouth like a slit,
With yellow teeth sticking out from it.
There was no red blood in his lips or skin,
He'd a sinister, hard, sharp soul within.
Perhaps, the thing that he most enjoyed
Was being rude when he felt annoyed.
He sucked his cane, he nodded to John,
He asked, "What's brought your lambkin on?"

John said, "I had meant to ask of you
Who's backing him, Dick; I hoped you knew."
Dick said, "Pill Stewart has placed the money.
I don't know whose."
                        John said, "That's funny."
"Why funny?" said Dick; but John said naught;
He looked at the horse's legs and thought.
Yet at last he said, "It beats me clean,
But whoever he is, he must be green.
There are eight in this could give him a stone,

And twelve should beat him on form alone.
The lad can ride, but it's more than riding
That will give the bay and the grey a hiding."

Dick sucked his cane and looked at the horse
With "Nothing's certain on Compton Course.
He looks a peach. Have you tried him high?"
John said, "You know him as well as I;
What he has done and what he can do.
He's been ridden to hounds this year or two.
When last he was raced, he made the running
For a stable companion twice at Sunning.
He was placed, bad third, in the Blowbury Cup,
And second at Tew with Kingston up.
He sulked at Folkstone, he funked at Speen,
He baulked at the ditch at Hampton Green.
Nick Kingston thought him a slug and cur,
'You must cut his heart out to make him stir.'
But his legs are iron; he's fine and fit."

Dick said, "Maybe; but he's got no grit.
With today's big field, on a course like this,
He will come to grief with that funk of his.

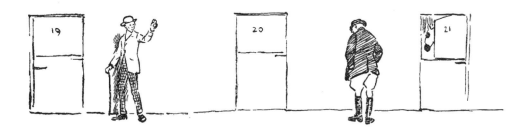

15

Well, it's queer, to me, that they've brought him on.
It's Kubbadar's race. Good-morning, John."

When Dick had gone from the stable-yard,
John wrote a note on a racing-card.
He said, "Since Stewart has placed the com.,
It's Mr. Cothill he got it from.
Now why should that nice young man go blind
And back his horse? Has he lost his mind?

Such a nice young fellow, so civil-spoken,
Should have more sense than to get him broken,
For broken he'll be as sure as eggs
If he puts his money on horses' legs.
And to trust to this, who's a nice old thing,
But can no more win than a cow can sing.
Well, they say that wisdom is dearly bought,
A world of pain for a want of thought;
But why should he back what stands no chance,
No more than the Rowley Mile's in France?
Why didn't he talk of it first with me?

Well, Lord, we trainers can let it be,
Why can't these owners abstain the same?
It can't be aught but a losing game.
He'll finish ninth; he'll be forced to sell
His horse, his stud, and his home as well;
He'll lose his lady, and all for this –
A daft belief in that horse of his.

It's nothing to me, a man might say,
That a rich young fool should be cast away,
Though what he does with his own, in fine,
Is certainly no concern of mine.
I'm paid to see that his horse is fit,
I can't engage for an owner's wit.
For the heart of a man may love his brother,
But who can be wise to save another?
Souls are our own to save from burning,
We must all learn how, and pay for learning.
And now, by the clock, that bell that went
Was the Saddling Bell for the first event.

Since the time comes close, it will save some swearing
If we get beforehand, and start preparing."

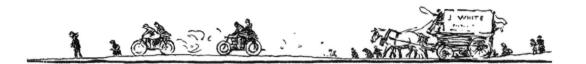

THE roads were filled with a drifting crowd,
Many mouth-organs droned aloud,
A couple of lads in scarlet hats,
Yellow trousers and purple spats,
Dragged their banjos, wearily eyeing
Passing brakes full of sportsmen Hi-ing.
Then with a long horn blowing a glory
Came the four-in-hand of the young Lord Tory,
The young Lord's eyes on his leaders' ears
And the blood-like team going by to cheers.
Then in a brake came cheerers and hooters
Peppering folk from tin peashooters;
The Green Man's Friendly in bright mauve caps
Followed fast in the Green Man's traps.
The crowd made way for the traps to pass,
Then a drum beat up with a blare of brass,
Medical students smart as paint
Sang gay songs of a sad complaint.

A wolf-eyed man who carried a kipe
Whistled as shrill as a man could pipe,
Then paused and grinned with his gaps of teeth
Crying, "Here's your colours for Compton Heath,
All the colours of all the starters,
For gentlemen's ties and ladies' garters;
Here you have them, penny a pin,
Buy your colours and see them win.
Here you have them, the favourites' own,
Sir Lopez' colours, the blue-white roan,
For all the races and what'll win 'em.
Real jockey's silk with a pin to pin 'em."

Out of his kipe he sold to many
Bright silk buttons and charged a penny.

A bookie walked with his clerk beside him,
His stool on his shoulders seemed to ride him,
His white top-hat bore a sign which ran
"Your old pal Bunkie the working man."
His clothes were a check of three-inch squares,
"Bright brown and fawn with the pearls in pairs."
Double pearl buttons ran down the side,
The knees were tight and the ankles wide.
A bright, thick chain made of discs of tin
Secured a board from his waist to chin.
The men in the brakes that passed at trot
Read "First past Post" and "Run or Not."
The bookie's face was an angry red,
His eyes seemed rolling inside his head.

His clerk was a lean man, secret, spare,
With thin lips knowing and damp black hair.
A big black bag much weathered with rain
Hung round his neck by a leathered chain.

Seven linked dancers singing a song
Bowed and kicked as they danced along,
The middleman thrust and pulled and squeezed
A concertina to tunes that pleased.
After them, honking, with Hey, Hey, Hey,
Came drivers thrusting to clear the way,
Drivers vexed by the concertina,
Saying "Go, bury that d----d hyena."
Drivers dusty with wind-red faces
Leaning out of their driving-places.
The dancers mocked them and called them names:
"Look at our butler," "Drive on, James."
The cars drove past and the dust rose after,
Little boys chased them yelling with laughter,
Clambering on them when they slowed
For a dirty ride down a perch of road.

A dark green car with a smart drab lining
Passed with a stately pair reclining;
Peering walkers standing aside
Saw Soyland's owner pass with his bride,
Young Sir Eustace, biting his lip,
Pressing his chin with his finger-tip.

Nerves on edge, as he could not choose,
From thought of the bets he stood to lose.
His lady, a beauty whom thought made pale,
Prayed from fear that the horse might fail.
A bright brass rod on the motor's bonnet
Carried her husband's colours on it,
Scarlet spots on a field of cream:
She stared ahead in a kind of dream.

Then came cabs from the railway stations,
Carrying men from all the nations,
Olive-skinned French with clipped moustaches,
Almond-eyed like Paris apaches.
Rosy French with their faces shining
From joy of living and love of dining.
Silent Spaniards, merry Italians,
Nobles, commoners, saints, rapscallions;
Russians tense with the quest of truth
That maddens manhood and saddens youth;
Learned Norwegians hale and limber,
Brown from the barques new in with timber.
Oregon men of six feet seven
With backs from Atlas and hearts from Heaven
Orleans Creoles, ready for duels,
Their delicate ears with scarlet jewels,
Green silk handkerchiefs round their throats,
In from sea with the cotton-boats.

Portuguese and Brazilianos,
Men from the mountains, men from the Llanos,
Men from the Pampas, men from the Sierras,
Men from the mines of the Cordilleras,
Men from the flats of the tropic mud
Where the butterfly glints his mail with blood;
Men from the pass where day by day
The sun's heat scales the rocks away;
Men from the hills where night by night
The sheep-bells give the heart delight;
Indians, Lascars and Bengalese,
Greeks from the mainland, Greeks from the seas;
All kinds of bodies, all kinds of faces,
All were coming to see the races,
Coming to see Sir Lopez run
And watch the English having their fun.

The Carib boxer from Hispaniola
Wore a rose in his tilted bowler;
He drove a car with a yellow panel,
He went full speed and he drove a channel.

Then came dog-carts and traps and wagons
With hampers of lunches, pies and flagons,
Bucks from city and flash young bloods
With vests "cut saucy" to show their studs,
Hawbuck Towler and Spicey Random
Tooled in style in a rakish tandem.

Blood Dick Haggit and Bertie Askins
Had dancers' skirts on their horses' gaskins;
Crash Pete Snounce with that girl of Dowser's
Drove a horse that was wearing trousers;
The wagonette from The Old Pier Head
Drove to the tune, "My Monkey's Dead."

The costermongers as smart as sparrows
Brought their wives in their donkey barrows.
The clean-legged donkeys, clever and cunning,
Their ears cocked forward, their neat feet running,
Their carts and harness flapping with flags,
Were bright as heralds and proud as stags.
And there in pride in the flapping banners
Were the costers' selves in blue bandannas,
And the costers' wives in feathers curling,
And their sons, with their sweet mouth-organs skirling.

And from midst of the road to the roadside shifting
The crowd of the world on foot went drifting,
Standing aside on the trodden grass
To chaff as they let the traffic pass.
Then back they flooded, singing and cheering,
Plodding forward and disappearing,
Up to the course to take their places,
To lunch and gamble and see the races.

The great Grand Stand, made grey by the weather,
Flaunted colours that tugged their tether;

Tier upon tier the wooden seats
Were packed as full as the London streets
When the King and Queen go by in state.

Click, click, clack, went the turnstile gate;
The orange-sellers cried "Fat and fine
Seville oranges, sweet, like wine:
Twopence apiece, all juice, all juice."
The pea and the thimble caught their goose.

Two white-faced lurchers, not over-clean,
Urged the passers to "spot the queen."
They flicked three cards that the world might choose,
They cried "All prizes. You cannot lose.
Come, pick the lady. Only a shilling."
One of their friends cried out, "I'm willing."
He "picked the lady" and took his pay,
And he cried, "It's giving money away."
Men came yelling "Cards of the races";
Men hawked matches and studs and laces;
Gipsy-women in green shawls dizened
Read girls' fortunes with eyes that glistened;
Negro minstrels on banjoes strumming
Sang at the stiles to people coming.

Like glistening beetles clustered close,
The myriad motors parked in rows,
The bonnets flashed, and the brass did clink,
As the drivers poured their motors drink.

The March wind blew the smell of the crowd,
All men there seemed crying aloud,
But over the noise a louder roar
Broke, as the wave that bursts on shore
Drowns the roar of the wave that comes,
So this roar rose on the lesser hums,
"I back the Field. I back the Field."

Man who lives under sentence sealed,
Tragical man, who has but breath
For few brief years as he goes to death,
Tragical man by strange winds blown
To live in crowds ere he die alone,
Came in his jovial thousands massing
To see Life moving and beauty passing.

They sucked their fruit in the wooden tiers
And flung the skins at the passers' ears;
Drumming their heels on the planks below,
They sang of Dolly of Idaho.

Past, like a flash, the first race went.

The time drew by to the great event.

AT a quarter to three the big bell pealed;
The horses trooped to the Saddling Field.
Covered in clothing, horse and mare
Pricked their ears at the people there;
Some showed devil, and some, composure,
As they trod their way to the great enclosure.

When the clock struck three and the men weighed out,
Charles Cothill shook, though his heart was stout.
The thought of his bets, so gaily laid,
Seemed a stone the more when he sat and weighed.

As he swung in the scales and nursed his saddle,
It seemed to him that his brains would addle;
For now that the plunger reached the brink,
The risk was more than he liked to think.

In ten more minutes his future life,
His hopes of home with his chosen wife,
Would all depend on a doubtful horse
In a crowded field over Compton Course.

He had backed Right Royal for all he owned.
At thought of his want of sense he groaned.
"All for a dream of the night," he thought.
He was right for weight at eleven naught.

Then Em's sweet face rose up in his brain,
He cursed his will that had dealt her pain:
To hurt sweet Emmy and lose her love
Was madman's folly by all above.

He saw too well as he crossed the yard
That his madman's plunge had borne her hard.
"To wring sweet Em like her drunken father,
I'd fall at the Pitch and end it rather.
Oh, I hope, hope, hope that her golden heart
Will give me a word before I start.
If I thought our love should have come to wreck,
I'd pull Right Royal and break my neck,
And Monkery's shoe might kick my brains out,
That my own heart's blood might wash my stains out.
But even if Emmy, my sweet, forgive,
I'm a ruined man, so I need not live,
For I've backed my horse with my all, by Heaven,
To be first in a field of thirty-seven,
And good as he is, the dream's a lie."

He saw no hope but to fall and die.

As he left the room for the Saddling Paddock
He looked as white as the flesh of haddock.

But Love, all seeing, though painted blind,
Makes wisdom live in a woman's mind.
His love knew well from her own heart's bleeding
The word of help that her man was needing;
And there she stood with her eyes most bright,
Ready to cheer her heart's delight.

She said, "My darling, I feel so proud
To see you followed by all the crowd;
And I shall be proud as I see you win.

Right Royal, Soyland and Peterkin
Are the three I pick, first, second, third.
And oh, now listen to what I heard.
Just now in the park Sir Norman Cooking
Said, 'Harding, how well Right Royal's looking.
They've brought him on in the ring, they say.'
John said, 'Sir Norman, today's his day.'
And Sir Norman said, 'If I had a monkey
I'd put it on yours, for he looks so spunky.'

So you see that the experts think as you.
Now, my own, own, own, may your dream come true,
As I know it will, as I know it must;
You have all my prayer and my love and trust.

29

Oh, one thing more that Sir Norman said,
'A lot of money has just been laid
On the mare Gavotte that no one knows.'
He said 'She's small, but, my word, she goes.
Since she bears no weight, if she only jumps,
She'll put these cracks to their ace of trumps.
But,' he said, 'she's slight for a course like this.'

That's all my gossip, so there it is.

Dear, reckon the words I spoke unspoken,
I failed in love and my heart is broken.

Now I go to my place to blush with pride
As the people talk of how well you ride;
I mean to shout like a bosun's mate
When I see you lead coming up the Straight.
Now may all God's help be with you, dear."

"Well, bless you, Em, for your words of cheer.
And now is the woodcock near the gin.
Good-bye.
            Now, Harding, we'd best begin."

At buckle and billet their fingers wrought,
Till the sheets were home and the bowlines taut.
As he knotted the reins and took his stand
The horse's soul came into his hand,
And up from the mouth that held the steel
Came an innermost word, half thought, half feel,
"My day today, O master, O master;
None shall jump cleaner, none shall go faster,

Call till you kill me, for I'll obey;
It's my day today, it's my day today."

In a second more he had found his seat,
And the standers-by jumped clear of feet,
For the big dark bay all fire and fettle
Had his blood in a dance to show his mettle.
Charles soothed him down till his tricks were gone;
Then he leaned for a find word from John.

John Harding's face was alert and grim,
From under his hand he talked to him.
"It's none of my business, sir," he said,
"What you stand to win or the bets you've made,
But the rumour goes that you've backed your horse.

Now you need no telling of Compton Course.
It's a dangerous course at the best of times,
But on days like this some jumps are crimes;
With a field like this, nigh forty starting,
After one time round it'll need re-charting.

Now think it a hunt, the first time round;
Don't think too much about losing ground,
Lie out of your ground, for sure as trumps
There'll be people killed in the first three jumps.
The second time round, pipe hands for boarding,
You can see what's doing and act according.

Now your horse is a slug and a sulker too,
Your way with the horse I leave to you;
But, sir, you watch for these jokers' tricks
And watch that devil on number six;
There's nothing he likes like playing it low,
What a horse mayn't like or a man mayn't know,
And what they love when they race a toff
Is to flurry his horse at taking off.
The ways of the crook are hard to learn.

Now watch that fence at the outer turn;
It looks so slight but it's highly like
That it's killed more men than the Dyers' Dyke.
It's down in a dip and you turn to take it,
And men in a bunch, just there, mistake it.
But well to the right, it's firmer ground,
And the quick way there is the long way round.
In Cannibal's year, in just this weather,
There were five came down at that fence together.
I called it murder, not riding races.

You've nothing to fear from the other places;
Your horse can jump.
                          Now I'll say no more.
They say you're on, as I said before.
It's none of my business, sir, but still
I would like to say that I hope you will.
Sir, I wish you luck. When we two next meet
I hope to hear how you had them beat."

Charles Cothill nodded with, "Thank you, John.
We'll try; and, oh, you're a thousand on."

He heard John's thanks, but knew at a glance
That John was sure that he stood no chance.

He turned Right Royal, he drew deep breath
With the thought, "Now for it; a ride to death.
Now come, my beauty, for dear Em's sake,
And if come you can't, may our necks both break."

And there to his front, with their riders stooping
For the final word, were the racers trooping.

Out at the gate to cheers and banter
They paced in pride to begin their canter.
Muscatel with the big white star,
The roan Red Ember, and Kubbadar,
Kubbadar with his teeth bared yellow
At the Dakkanese, his stable-fellow.
Then Forward-Ho, then a chestnut weed,
Skysail, slight, with a turn of speed.
The neat Gavotte under black and coral,
Then the Mutineer, Lord Leybourne's sorrel,
Natuna mincing, Syringa sidling,
Stormalong fighting to break his bridling,
Thunderbolt dancing with raw nerves quick,
Trying a savage at Bitter Dick.
The Ranger (winner three years before),
Now old, but ready for one try more;
Hadrian; Thankful; the stable-cronies,
Peterkinooks and Dear Adonis;
The flashing Rocket, with taking action;
Exception, backed by the Tencombe faction;
Old Sir Francis and young King Tony,
And gaunt Path Finder with great hips bony.

At this, he rode through the open gate
Into the course to try his fate.

He heard a roar from a moving crowd;
Right Royal kindled and cried aloud.
There was the course, stand, rail and pen,
Peopled with seventy thousand men;
Seventy thousand faces staring,
Carriages parked, a brass band blaring:
Over the stand the flags in billows
Bent their poles like the wands of willows.
All men there seemed trying to bawl,
Yet a few great voices topped them all:
"I back the Field! I back the Field!"

Right Royal trembled with pride and squealed.

Charles Cothill smiled with relief to find
This roaring crowd to his horse's mind.

He passed the stand where his lady stood;
His nerves were tense to the multitude;
His blood beat hard and his eyes grew dim
As he knew that some were cheering him.
Then, as he turned, at his pace's end
There came a roar as when floods descend.
All down the Straight from the crowded stands
Came the yells of voices and clap of hands,
For with bright bay beauty that shone like flame
The favourite horse, Sir Lopez, came.

His beautiful hips and splendid shoulders
And power of stride moved all beholders,
Moved non-betters to try to bet
On that favourite horse not beaten yet.
With glory of power and speed he strode
To a sea of cheering that moved and flowed
And followed and heaped and burst like storm
From the joy of men in the perfect form:
Cheers followed his path both sides the course.

Charles Cothill sighed when he saw that horse.

The cheering died, then a burst of clapping
Met Soyland's coming all bright from strapping,
A big dark brown who was booted thick
Lest one of the jumps should make him click.
He moved very big, he'd a head like a fiddle,
He seemed all ends without any middle,
But ill as he looked, that outcast racer
Was a rare good horse and a perfect 'chaser.

Then The Ghost came on, then Meringue, the bay,
Then proud Grey Glory, the dapple-grey;
The splendid grey brought a burst of cheers.
Then Cimmeroon, who had tried for years
And had thrice been placed and had once been fourth,
Came trying again the proverb's worth.

Then again, like a wave as it runs a pier,
On and on, unbroken, there came a cheer
As Monkery, black as a collier-barge,
Trod sideways, bickering, taking charge.
Cross-Molin, from the Blowbury, followed,
Lucky Shot skipped, Coranto wallowed,
Then Counter Vair, the declared-to-win,
Stable-fellow of Cross-Molin;
Culverin last, with Cannonade,
Formed rearguard to the grand parade.

And now, as they turned to go to post,
The Skysail calfishly barged The Ghost,
The Ghost lashed out with a bitter knock
On the tender muscle of Skysail's hock,
And Skysail's hope of that splendid hour
Was cut off short like a summer flower.
From the cantering crowd he limped apart
Back to the Paddock and did not start.

As they cantered down, Charles Cothill's mind
Was filled with joy that his horse went kind;
He showed no sulks, no sloth, no fear,
But leant on his rein and pricked his ear.

They lined themselves at the post to start,
Charles took his place with a thumping heart.

Excitement running in waves took hold,
His teeth were chattered, his hands were cold,
His joy to be there was mixed with dread
To be left at post when they shot ahead.
The horses sparred as though drunk with wine,
They bickered and snatched at taking line.

Then a grey-haired man with a hawk-like face

Read from a list each rider's place.
Sitting astride his pommely hack,
He ordered them up or sent them back;
He bade them heed that they jump their nags
Over every jump between the flags.
Here Kubbadar, who was pulling double,
Went sideways, kicking and raising trouble,
Monkery seconded, kicking and biting,
Thunderbolt followed by starting fighting.

The starter eyed them and gave the order
That the three wild horses keep the border,
With men to hold them to keep them quiet.
Boys from the stables stopped their riot.
Out of the line to the edge of the field
The three wild biters and kickers wheeled;
Then the rest edged up and pawed and bickered,
Reached at their reins and snatched and snickered,
Flung white foam as they stamped their hate
Of passionate blood compelled to wait.

Then the starter shouted to Charles, "Good heaven,
This isn't a circus, you on Seven."
For Royal squirmed like a box of tricks
And Coranto's rider, the number Six,
Cursed at Charles for a green young fool
Who ought to be at a riding school.
After a minute of swerves and shoving,
A line like a half-moon started moving;
Then Rocket and Soyland leaped to stride,
To be pulled up short and wheeled to side.

Then the trickier riders started thrusting,
Judging the starter's mind too trusting;
But the starter said, "You know quite clearly
That isn't allowed; though you'd like it dearly."

Then Cannonade made a sideways bolt
That gave Exception an ugly jolt.
Then the line, reformed, broke all to pieces.

Then the line reforms, and the tumult ceases.
Each man sits tense though his racer dances;
In a slow, jerked walk the line advances.

And then in a flash, more felt than seen,
The flag shot down and the course showed green,
And the line surged forwards and all that glory
Of speed was sweeping to make a story.

One second before, Charles Cothill's mind
Had been filled with fear to be left behind,
But now with a rush, as when hounds leave cover,
The line broke up and his fear was over.
A glimmer of bay behind The Ghost
Showed Dear Adonis still there at post.

Out to the left, a joy to his backer,
Kubbadar led the field a cracker,
The thunder of horses, all fit and foaming,
Made the blood not care whether death were coming.
A glimmer of silks, blue, white, green, red,
Flashed into his eye and went ahead;
Then hoof-casts scattered, then rushing horses
Passed at his side with all their forces.
His blood leapt up, but his mind said "No,
Steady, my darling, slow, go slow.
In the first time round this ride's a hunt."

The Turk's Grave Fence made a line in front.

Long years before, when the race began,
That first of the jumps had maimed a man;
His horse, the Turk, had been killed and buried
There in the ditch by horse-hoofs herried;
And over the poor Turk's bones at pace
Now, every year, there goes the race,
And many a man makes doctor's work
At the thorn-bound ditch that hides the Turk,
And every man as he rides that course
Thinks, there, of the Turk, that good old horse.

The thick thorn-fence stands five feet high,
With a ditch beyond unseen by eye,
Which a horse must guess from his urgent rider
Pressing him there to jump it wider.

And being so near both Stand and Post,
Out of all the jumps men haunt it most,
And there, with the crowd, and the undulled nerves,
The old horse balks and the young horse swerves,
And the good horse falls with the bad on top
And beautiful boldness comes to stop.

Charles saw the rush of the leading black,
And the forehands lift and the men sway back;
He steadied his horse, then with crash and crying
The top of the Turk's Grave Fence went flying.
Round in a flash, refusing danger,
Came the Lucky Shot right into Ranger;
Ranger swerving knocked Bitter Dick,
Who blundered at it and leaped too quick;
Then crash went blackthorn as Bitter Dick fell,
Meringue jumped on him and rolled as well.
As Charles got over he splashed the dirt
Of the poor Turk's grave on two men hurt.

Right Royal landed. With cheers and laughter
Some horses passed him and some came after;
A fine brown horse strode up beside him,
It was Thankful running with none to ride him;
Thankful's rider, dizzy and sick,
Lay in the mud by Bitter Dick.
In front was the curving street of Course,
Barred black by the leaps unsmashed by horse.

A cloud blew by and the sun shone bright,
Showing the guard-rails gleaming white.
Little red flags, that gusts blew tense,
Streamed to the wind at each black fence.

And smiting the turf to clods that scattered
Was the rush of the race, the thing that mattered,
A tide of horses in fury flowing,
Beauty of speed in glory going,
Kubbadar pulling, romping first,
Like a big black fox that had made his burst.

And away and away and away they went,
A visible song of what life meant.
Living in houses, sleeping in bed,
Going to business, all seemed dead,
Dead as death to that rush in strife,
Pulse for pulse with the heart of life.

"For to all," Charles thought, "when the blood beats high
Comes the glimpse of that which may not die;
When the world is stilled, when the wanting dwindles,
When the mind takes light and the spirit kindles,
One stands on a peak of this old earth."

Charles eyed his horses and sang with mirth.
What of this world that spins through space?
With red blood running he rode a race,
The beast's red spirit was one with his,
Emulous and in ecstasies;

Joy that from heart to wild heart passes
In the wild things going through the grasses;
In the hares in the corn, in shy gazelles
Running the sand where no man dwells;
In horses scared at the prairie spring;
In the dun deer noiseless, hurrying;
In fish in the dimness scarcely seen,
Save as shadows shooting in a shaking green;
In birds in the air, neck-straining, swift,
Wing touching wing while no wings shift,
Seen by none, but when stars appear
A reaper wandering home may hear
A sigh aloft where the stars are dim,
Then a great rush going over him:
This was his; it had linked him close
To the force by which the comet goes,
With the rein none sees, with the lash none feels,
But with fire-mane tossing and flashing heels.

The roar of the race-course died behind them,
In front were their Fates, they rode to find them,
With the wills of men, with the strengths of horses,
They dared the minute with all their forces.

PART II

STILL pulling double, black Kubbadar led,
Pulling his rider half over his head;
Soyland's cream jacket was spotted with red,
Spotted with dirt from the rush of their tread.

Bright bay Sir Lopez, the loveliest there,
Galloped at ease as though taking the air,
Well in his compass with plenty to spare.
Gavotte and The Ghost and the brown Counter Vair
Followed him close with Syringa the mare,
And the roan horse Red Ember, who went like a hare,
And Forward-Ho bolting, though his rider did swear.

Keeping this order, they reached the next fence,
Which was living plashed blackthorn with gorse-toppings dense;

47

In the gloom of its darkness it loomed up immense.
And Forward-Ho's glory had conquered his sense
And he rushed it, not rising, and never went thence.
And down in the ditch where the gorse-spikes were scattered
That bright chestnut's soul from his body was shattered,
And his rider shed tears on the dear head all spattered.

King Tony came down, but got up with a stumble,
His rider went sideways, but knew how to tumble,
And got up and remounted, though the pain made him humble,
And he rode fifty yards and then stopped in a fumble.

With a rush and a crashing Right Royal went over
With the stride of a stalwart and the blood of a lover,
He landed on stubble now pushing with clover,

And just as he landed, the March sun shone bright
And the blue sky showed flamelike and the dun clouds turned white;
The little larks panted aloft their delight,
Trembling and singing as though one with the light.

And Charles, as he rode, felt the joy of their singing,
While over the clover the horses went stringing,
And up from Right Royal the message came winging,
"It is my day today, though the pace may be stinging,
Though the jumps be all danger and the going all clinging."
The white, square church-tower with its weather-cock swinging
Rose up on the right above grass and dark plough,
Where the elm trees' black branches had bud on the bough.

Riderless Thankful strode on at his side,
His bright stirrup-irons flew up at each stride;
Being free, in this gallop, had filled him with pride.
Charles thought, "What would come if he ran out or shied?
I wish from my heart that the brute would keep wide."
Coranto drew up on Right Royal's near quarter,
Beyond lay a hurdle and ditch full of water.

And now as they neared it, Right Royal took heed
Of the distance to go and the steps he would need;
He cocked to the effort with eyes bright as gleed,
Then Coranto's wide wallow shot past him at speed:
His rider's "Hup, hup, now!" called out quick and cheerly,
Sent him over in style, but Right Royal jumped early,

Just a second too soon, and from some feet too far,
Charles learned the mistake as he struck the top bar;
Then the water flashed skywards, the earth gave a jar,
And the man on Coranto looked back with "Aha!

That'll teach you, my son." Then with straining of leather,
Grey Glory and Monkery landed together.

For a second the stunning kept Charles from his pain,
Then his sense flooded back, making everything plain.
He was down in the mud, but he still held the rein;
Right Royal was heaving his haunch from the drain.
The field was ahead of him, going like rain,
And though the plough held them, they went like the wind
To the eyes of a man left so badly behind.

Charles climbed to his feet as Right Royal crawled out,
He said, "That's extinction beyond any doubt."
On the plough, on and on, went the rush of the rout.
Charles mounted and rode, for his courage was stout,
And he would not give in till the end of the bout,
But plastered with poachings he rode on forsaken:
He had lost thirty lengths and his horse had been shaken.

Across the wet ploughland he took a good pull,
With the thought that the cup of his sorrow was full,
For the speed of a stag and the strength of a bull
Could hardly recover the ground he had lost.

Right Royal went dully, then snorted and tost,

Tost his head, with a whicker, went on, and went kind,
And the horse's great spirit touched Charles in the mind.
Though his bruise made him dizzy and tears made him blind,
He would try to the finish, and so they should find.
He was last, thirty lengths. Here he took in his sails,
For the field had come crash at the white post and rails.

Here Sir Francis ran out, scaring all who stood near,
Going crash through the rail like a runaway deer,
Then the riderless Thankful upset Mutineer,
Dakkanese in refusing, wheeled round like a top
Into Culverin's shoulder, which made them both stop.

They reeled from the shock, slithered sideways, and crashed,
Dakkanese on the guard-rail, which gave, and then smashed.
As he rolled, the near shoes of the Culverin flashed
High in air for a moment, bright iron in strain:
Then he rose with no rider and tripped in his rein.

Right Royal came up as the Dakkanese rose
All trembling and cowed as though beaten with blows;
The Culverin stumbled with the reins in his toes;
On the far side the leap stood the Mutineer grazing,
His man was a heap which some fellows were raising.

Right Royal strode on, through a second wet plough,
With the field far ahead (Kubbadar in the bow).
Charles thought, "Kubbadar's got away from him now.
Well, it's little to me, for they're so far ahead
That they'll never come back, though I ride myself dead."

Right Royal bored forward and leaned on his hand,
"Good boy," said his master. "He must understand.
You're the one friend I'll have when I've sold all my land
God pity my Em as we come past the Stand,
Last of all, and all muddy; but now for Jim's Pitch."
Four feet of gorse fence, then a fifteen-foot ditch.

And the fifteen-foot ditch glittered bright to the brim
With the brook that ran through it where the grayling did swim;
In the shallows it sparkled, in the deeps it was dim,
When the race was first run it had nearly drowned Jim,
And now the bright irons of twenty-four horses
Were to flicker its ripples with knockings of gorses.

From far in the rear Charles could watch them take hold
Of their horses and push them across the light mould;
How their ears all cocked forward, how the drumming hoofs rolled!
Kubbadar, far ahead, flew across like a bird,
Then Soyland, bad second, with Muscatel third.

Then Sir Lopez, and Path Finder, striding alone,

Then the good horse, Red Ember, the fleabitten roan.
Then the little Gavotte bearing less than ten stone.
Then a crowd of all colours with Peterkinooks
Going strong as a whale goes, head up and out flukes.

And there, as Charles watched, as the shoulders went back,
The riderless Thankful swerved left off the track,
Crossing just to the front of the Cimmeroon black.
Ere the rider could see what his horse was about,
Cimmeroon swerved, like Thankful, and followed him out.

Across the great grass in the midst of the course
Cimmeroon ran a match with the riderless horse,
Then the rider took charge, part by skill, part by force;
He turned Cimmeroon to re-enter the race
Seven lengths behind Charles in the post of disgrace.

Beyond the next fence, at the top of a slope,
Charles saw his field fading and gave up all hope.
Yet he said, "Any error will knot me my rope.
I wish that some power would help me to see
What would give the best chance for Right Royal and me.

Shall I hurry downhill, to catch up when I can ?
Being last is the devil for horse and for man,
For it makes the horse slack and it makes the man sick.
Well, I've got to decide and I've got to be quick.

I had better catch up, for if I should be last,
It would kill my poor Emmy to see me come past.
I cannot leave Emmy to suffer like that,
So I'll hurry downhill and then pull on the flat."

So he thought, so he settled, but then, as he stirred,
Right Royal's ears moved like a vicious man's word;
So he thought, "If I try it, the horse will refuse."
So he gave up the project and shook in his shoes.

Then he thought, "Since the horse will not stand interference,
I must even sit quiet and sink the appearance,
Since his nerves have been touched, it's as well we're alone."
He turned down the hill with his heart like a stone.

"But," he cried, "they'll come back, for they've gone such a burst
That they'll all soon be panting, in need to be nursed,
They will surely come back, but to wait till they do,
Lord, it's hell to the waiter, it cuts a man through."

Then into his mind came the Avalon case,
When a man, left at post, without hope of a place,
First had suffered in patience, then had wormed his way up,
Then had come with fine judgment, and just won the Cup.

Hoofs thundered behind him, the Cimmeroon caught him,
His man cursing Thankful and the sire who wrought him.
"Did you see that brown devil?" he cried as he passed;
"He carried me out, but I'll never be last.

Just the wrong side the water the brute gave a swerve,
And he carried me out, half across the course-curve.
Look, he's cut right across now, we'll meet him again.
Well, I hope someone knocks him and kicks out his brain.

Well, I'll never be last, though I can't win the Cup.
No sense lolling here, man, you'd better pull up."
Then he roused Cimmeroon, and was off like a swallow.
Charles watched, sick at heart, with a longing to follow.

"Better follow," he thought, "for he knows more than I,
Since he rode here before, and it's wiser to try:
Would my horse had but wings, would his feet would but lift;
Would we spun on this speedway as wind spins the drift.

There they go out of sight, over fence, to the Turn;
They are going still harder, they leave me astern.
They will never come back, I am lost past recall."
So he cried for a comfort, and only gat gall.

In the glittering branches of the world without end
Were the spirits, Em's Helper and Charles Cothill's Friend,
And the Force of Right Royal with a crinier of flame;
There they breathed the bright glory till the summoning came.

From the Stand where Em watched, from the field where Charles rode,
From the mud where Right Royal in solitude strode,
Came the call of three spirits to the spirits that guard,
Crying, "Up now, and help him, for the danger bears hard."

There they looked, those immortals, from the boughs dropping balm,
But their powers were stirred not, and their grave brows were calm,
For they said, "He's despairing and the horse is still vext."
Charles cleared Channing's Blackthorn and strode to the next.

The next was the Turn in a bogland of rushes;
There the springs of still water were trampled to slushes;
The peewits lamented, flapping down, flagging far,
The riders dared death wards each trusting his star.

The mud made them slither, the Turn made them close,
The stirrup steels clinked as they thrust in their toes,
The brown horse Exception was struck as he rose,
Struck to earth by the Rocket, then kicked by the grey,
Then Thunderbolt smote him and rolled him astray.

The man on Exception, Bun Manor, fell clear,
With Monkery's shoes half an inch from his ear,
A drench of wet mud from the hoofs struck his cheek,
But the race was gone from him before he could speak.

There Exception and Thunderbolt ended their race,
Their bright flanks all smeared with the mud of the place;
In the green fields of Tencombe and the grey downs of Churn
Their names had been glories till they fell at the Turn.

Em prayed in her place that her lover might know
Not to hurry Right Royal, but let him go slow:
White-lipped from her praying, she sat, with shut eyes,
Begging help from her Helper, the deathless, the wise.

From the gold of his branches her Helper took heed,
He sent forth a thought to help Charles in his need.
As the white, gleaming gannet eyes fish in the sea,
So the Thought sought a mortal to bring this to be.

By the side of Exception Bun Manor now stood,
Sopping rags on a hock that was dripping bright blood.
He had known Charles of old and defeat made him kind,
The thought from the Helper came into his mind.

So he cried to Charles Cothill, "Go easy," he cried,
"Don't hurry; don't worry; sit still and keep wide.
They flowed like the Severn, they'll ebb like the tide.
They'll come back and you'll catch them." His voice died away.
In front lay the Dyke, deep as drowning, steel grey.

Charles felt his horse see it and stir at the sight.
Again his heart beat to the dream of the night;
Once again in his heart's blood the horse seemed to say,
"I'll die or I'll do it. It's my day today."

He saw the grey water in shade from its fence,
The rows of white faces all staring intense;
All the heads straining forward, all the shoulders packt dense.
Beyond, he saw Thankful, the riderless brown,
Snatching grass, dodging capture, with reins hanging down.

Then Thankful stopped eating and cocked up his head,
He eyed the swift horses that Kubbadar led,
His eye filled with fire at the roll of their tread;
Then he tore down the course with a flash of bright shoes,
As the race's bright herald on fire with news.

As Charles neared the water, the Rocket ran out
By jumping the railings and kicking a clout
Of rotten white woodwork to startle the trout.
When Charles cleared the water, the grass stretcht before
And the glory of going burned in to the core.

Far over his head with a whicker of wings
Came a wisp of five snipe from a field full of springs;
The gleam on their feathers went wavering past
And then some men booed him for being the last.

But last though he was, all his blood was on fire
With the rush of the wind and the gleam of the mire,
And the leap of his heart to the skylarks in quire,
And the feel of his horse going onward, on, on,
Under sky with white banners and bright sun that shone.

Like a star in the night, like a spring in the waste,
The image of Emmy rose up as he raced,
Till his mind was made calm and his spirit was braced.
For the prize was bright Emmy; his blood beat and beat
As her beauty made music in that thunder of feet.

60

The wind was whirled past him, it hummed in his ears,
Right Royal's excitement had banished his fears,
For his leap was like singing, his stride was like cheers,
All his blood was in glory, all his soul was blown bare,
They were one, blood and purpose, they strode through the air.

"What is life if I lose her, what is death if I win?
At the end of this living the new lives begin.
Whatever life may be, whatever death is,
I am spirit eternal, I am this, I am this!"

Girls waved, and men shouted, like flashes, like shots,
Out of pale blurs of faces whose features were dots;
Two fences with toppings were cleared without hitch,
Then they ran for Lost Lady's, a fence and dry ditch.

Here Monkery's rider, on seeing a chance,
Shot out beyond Soyland to lead the advance.
Then he steadied and summed up his field with a glance.
All crossed the Lost Lady's, that dry ditch of fear,
Then a roar broke about them, the race-course was near.

Right and left were the swing-boats and merry-go-rounds,
Yellow varnish that wavered, machines making sounds,
Shots cracking like cork-pops, fifes whining with steam,
"All hot," from a pieman; all blurred as in dream;

Then the motors, then cheering, then the brass of a band,
Then the white rails all crowded with a mob on each hand.
Then they swerved to the left over gorse-bush and hurdle
And they rushed for the Water, where a man's blood might curdle.

Charles entered the race-course and prayed in his mind
That love for the moment might make Emmy blind,
Not see him come past half a distance behind:
For an instant he thought, "I must shove on ahead,
For to pass her like this, Lord, I'd rather be dead."

Then, in crossing the hurdle, the Stand arose plain,
All the flags, horns and cheers beat like blows on his brain,
And he thought, "Time to race when I come here again,
If I once lose my head, I'll be lost past appeal."
All the crowd flickered past, like a film on a reel,

Like a ribbon, whirled past him, all painted with eyes.
All the real, as he rode, was the horse at his thighs,
And the thought, "They'll come back, if I've luck, if I'm wise."
Some banners uncrumpled on the blue of the skies,
The cheers became frantic, the blur of men shook,
As Thankful and Kubbadar went at the brook.

Neck and neck, stride for stride, they increased as they neared it,
Though the danger gleamed greyly, they galloped to beard it;
And Kubbadar dwelt on his jump as he cleared it,
While Thankful went on with a half a length lead.
Charles thought, "Kubbadar, there, is going to seed."

Then Monkery took it, then Soyland, then two,
Muscatel and Sir Lopez, who leaped not but flew,
Like a pair of June swallows going over the dew,
Like a flight of bright fishes from a field of seas blue,
Like a wisp of snipe wavering in the dusk out of view.
Then Red Ember, Path Finder, Gavotte and Coranto,
Then The Ghost going level by Syringa a-taunto.

Then Peterkinooks, then the Cimmeroon black,
Who had gone to his horses, not let them come back;
Then Stormalong rousing, then the Blowbury crack,
Counter Vair, going grandly beside Cross-Molin,
All charged the bright brook and Coranto went in.

Natuna, Grey Glory and Hadrian followed,
Flying clear of the water where Coranto now wallowed;
Cannonade leaped so big that the lookers-on holloed.
Ere the splash from Coranto was bright on the grass,
The face of the water had seen them all pass.

But Coranto half scrambled, then slipped on his side,
Then churned in the mud till the brook was all dyed;

As Charles reached the water Coranto's man cried,
"Put him at it like blazes and give him a switch;
Jump big, man, for God's sake, I'm down in the ditch."

Right Royal went at it and streamed like a comet,
And the next thing Charles knew, he was twenty yards from it;
And he thought about Em as he rushed past her place,
With a prayer for God's peace on her beautiful face.

Then he tried to keep steady. "Oh, steady," he said,
"I'm riding with judgment, not leading a raid,
And I'm getting excited, and there's Cannonade.
What's the matter?" he shouted as Royal swept past.
"Sprained!" shouted the man; "over-jumped, at the last."

"Rough luck," shouted Charles. Then the crowd dropped away,
Then the sun shone behind him, the bright turned to grey;
They were round, the first time, they were streaming away
For the second time round. There the starting-post shone.
Then they swung round the curve and went galloping on.

All the noise died behind, Fate was waiting in front,
Now the racing began, they had done with the hunt.
With the sunlight behind him Charles saw how they went;
No nearer, but further, and only one spent.

Only Kubbadar dwelling, the rest going strong,
Taking jump after jump as a bird takes a song,
Their thirty lengths' lead seemed a weary way long,
It seemed to grow longer, it seemed to increase:
"This is bitter," he said. "May it be for my peace.

My dream was a glimpse of the world beyond sense,
All beauty and wisdom are messages thence.
There the difference of bodies and the strain of control
Are removed; beast with man speaks, and spirit with soul.

My vision: was Wisdom, or the World as it Is.
Fate rules us, not Wisdom, whose ways are not his,
Fate, weaponed with all things, has willed that I fall;
So be it, Fate orders, and we go to the wall.

Go down to the beaten, who have come to the truth
That is deeper than sorrow and stronger than youth,
That is God, the foundation, who sees and is just
To the beauty within us who are nothing but dust.

Yet, Royal, my comrade, before Fate decides,
His hand stays, uncertain, like the sea between tides,
Then a man has a moment, if he strike not too late,
When his soul shakes the world-soul, and can even change Fate.

So you and I, Royal, before we give in,
Will spend blood and soul in our effort to win,
And if all be proved vain when our effort is sped,
May the hoofs of our conquerors trample us dead."

Then the soul of Right Royal thrilled up through each hand:
"We are one, for this gallop; we both understand.
If my lungs give me breathing, if my loins stand the strain,
You may lash me to strips and it shan't be in vain.

For today, in this hour, my Power will come
From my Past to my Present (and a Spirit gives some).
We have gone many gallops, we two, in the past,
When I go with my Power you will know me at last.

You remember the morning when the red leaf hung still,
When they found in the beech-clump on Lollingdon Hill,
When we led past the Sheep Fold and along the Fair Mile?
When I go with my Power, that will not seem worth while.

Then the day in the valley when we found in the wood,
When we led all the gallop to the river in flood,
And the sun burst out shining as the fox took the stream;
When I go with my Power, that will all seem a dream.

Then the day on the Downland when we went like the light
From the spring by Hurst Compton till the Clump was in sight,
Till we killed by The Romans, where Blowbury is;
All the best of that gallop shall be nothing to this.

If I failed in the past with my Power away,
I was only my shadow, it was not my day,
So I sulked like my sire, or shrank, like my dam;
Now I come to my Power you will know what I am.

I've the strength, you've the brain, we are running as one,
And nothing on earth can be lost till it's won.
If I live to the end naught shall put you to shame."
So he thrilled, going flame-like, with a crinier of flame.

"Yet," he thrilled, "it may be, that before the end come
Death will touch me, the Changer, and carry me home.
For we know not, O master, when our life shall have rest,
But the Life is near change that has uttered its best.
If we grow like the grasses, we fall like the flower,
And I know, I touch Death when I come to my Power."

Now over the course flew invisible birds,
All the wants of the watchers, all the thoughts and winged words,
Swift as floatings of fire from a bonfire's crest
When they burn leaves on Kimble and the fire streams west,

Bright an instant, then dying, but renewed and renewed,
So the thoughts chased the racers like hounds that pursued,
Bringing cheer to their darlings, bringing curse to their foes,
Searching into men's spirits till their Powers arose.

Red and rigid the Powers of the riding men were,
And as sea birds on Ailsa, in the nesting time there,
Rise like leaves in a whirlwind and float like leaves blown,
So the wants chased the riders and fought for their own.

Unseen by the riders, from the myriad tense brains
Came the living thoughts flying to clutch at men's reins,
Clearing paths for their darlings by running in cry
At the heads of their rivals till the darlings gat by,

As in football, when forwards heave all in a pack,
With their arms round each other and their heels heeling back,
And their bodies all straining, as they heave, and men fall,
And the halves hover hawklike to pounce on the ball,

And the runners poise ready, while the mass of hot men
Heaves and slips, like rough bullocks making play in a pen,
And the crowd sees the heaving, and is still, till it break,
So the riders endeavoured as they strained for the stake.

They skimmed through the grassland, they came to the plough,
The wind rushed behind them like the waves from a prow,
The clods rose behind them with speckles of gold
From the iron-crusht coltsfoot flung up from the mould.

ALL green was the plough with the thrusts of young corn,
Pools gleamed in the ruts that the cart-wheels had worn,
And Kubbadar's man wished he had not been born.
Natuna was weary and dwelt on her stride,
Grey Glory's grey tail rolled about, side to side.

Then swish, came a shower, from a driving grey cloud,
Though the blue sky shone brightly and the larks sang aloud.

As the squall of rain pelted, the coloured caps bowed,
With Thankful still leading and Monkery close,
The hoofs smacked the clayland, the flying clods rose.

They slowed on the clayland, the rain pelted by,
The end of a rainbow gleamed out in the sky;
Natuna dropped back till Charles heard her complain,
Grey Glory's forequarters seemed hung on his rein,
Cimmeroon clearly was feeling the strain.
But the little Gavotte skimmed the clay like a witch,
Charles saw her coquet as she went at Jim's Pitch.

They went at Jim's Pitch, through the deeply dug gaps
Where the hoofs of great horses had kicked off the scraps.
And there at the water they met with mishaps,
For Natuna stopped dead and Grey Glory went in,
And a cannon on landing upset Cross-Molin.

As swallows bound northward when apple-bloom blows,
See laggards drop spent from their flight as it goes,
Yet can pause not in heaven as they scythe the thin air
But go on to the house-eaves and the nests clinging bare,
So Charles flashed beyond them, those three men the less
Who had gone to get glory and met with distress.

He rode to the rise-top, and saw, down the slope,
The race far ahead at a steady strong lope
Going over the grassland, too well for his peace,
They were steady as oxen and strong as wild geese.

70

As a man by a cornfield on a windy wild day
Sees the corn bow in shadows ever hurrying away,
And wonders, in watching, when the light with bright feet
Will harrow those shadows from the ears of the wheat,
So Charles, as he watched, wondered when the bright face
Of the finish would blaze on that smouldering race.

ON the last of the grass, ere the going was dead,
Counter Vair's man shot out with his horse by the head,
Like a partridge put up from the stubble he sped,
He dropped Kubbadar and he flew by Red Ember
Up to Monkery's girth like a leaf in November.

Then Stormalong followed, and went to the front,
And just as the find puts a flame to a hunt,
So the rush of those horses put flame to the race.
Charles saw them all shaken to quickening pace.

And Monkery moved, not to let them go by,
And the steadiest rider made ready to fly;
Well into the wet land they leaped from the dry,
They scattered the rain-pools that mirrored the sky,
They crushed down the rushes that pushed from the plough.
And Charles longed to follow, but muttered "Not now."

"Not now," so he thought. "Yet if not" (he said) "when
Shall I come to those horses and scupper their men?
Will they never come back? Shall I never get up?"
So he drank bitter gall from a very cold cup.

But he nursed his horse gently and prayed for the best,
And he caught Cimmeroon, who was sadly distrest,
And he passed Cimmeroon, with the thought that the black
Was as nearly dead beat as the man on his back.
Then he gained on his field who were galled by the churn,
The plough searched them out as they came to the Turn.

But Gavotte, black and coral, went strong as a spate;
Charles thought, "She's a flier and she carries no weight."

And now, beyond question, the field began tailing,
For all had been tested and many were ailing,
The riders were weary, the horses were failing,
The blur of bright colours rolled over the railing,
With the grunts of urged horses, and the oaths of hot men,
"Gerr on, you," "Come on, now," agen and agen;
They spattered the mud on the willow tree's bole
And they charged at the danger; and the danger took toll.

For Monkery landed, but dwelt on the fence,
So that Counter Vair passed him in galloping thence.
Then Stormalong blundered, then bright Muscatel
Slipped badly on landing and stumbled and fell,
Then rose in the morrish, with his man on his neck
Like a nearly dead sailor afloat on a wreck,
With his whip in the mud and his stirrups both gone,
Yet he kept in the saddle and made him go on.

As Charles leaped the Turn, all the field was tailed out
Like petals of roses that wind blows about,
Like petals of colour blown back and brought near,
Like poppies in wind-flaws when corn is in ear;
Fate held them or sped them, the race was beginning.
Charles said, "I must ride, or I've no chance of winning."

So gently he quickened, yet making no call;
Right Royal replied as though knowing it all.
He passed Kubbadar, who was ready to fall,
Then he strode up to Hadrian, up to his girth,
They eyed the Dyke's glitter and picked out a berth.
Now the race reached the water and over it flew
In a sweep of great muscle strained taut and guyed true.
There Muscatel floundered and came to a halt,
Muscatel, the bay 'chaser without any fault.

Right Royal's head lifted, Right Royal took charge,
On the left near the railings, ears cocked, going large,
Leaving Hadrian behind as a yacht leaves a barge.
Though Hadrian's rider called something unheard,
He was past him at speed like the albatross bird,
Running up to Path Finder, they leaped, side by side,
And the foam from Path Finder flecked white on his hide.

And on landing, he lifted, while Path Finder dwelt,
And his noble eye brightened from the glory he felt,
And the mud flung behind him flicked Path Finder's chest,
As he left him behind and went on to the rest.

Charles cast a glance back, but he could not divine
Why the man on Path Finder should make him a sign,
Nor why Hadrian's rider should shout, and then point,
With his head nodded forward and a jerked elbow joint.

But he looked as he pointed, both forward and down,
And he saw that Right Royal was smeared like a clown,
Smeared red and bespattered with flecks of bright blood,
From a blood-vessel burst, as he well understood.

And just as he saw it, Right Royal went strange
As one whom Death's finger has touched to a change;
He went with a stagger that sickened the soul,
As a force stricken feeble and out of control.

Charles thought, "He is dying, and this is the end,

I am losing my Emmy and killing my friend;
He was hurt when we fell, as I thought at the first,
And I've forced him three miles with a blood-vessel burst!

And his game heart went on." Here a rush close behind
Made him cast a glance back with despair in his mind.
It was Cimmeroon rushing, his lips twitcht apart,
His eyes rolled back sightless, and death in his heart.
He reached to Right Royal, then fell, and was dead,
Nevermore to stretch reins with his beautiful head.

A gush of bright blood filled his mouth as he sank,
And he reached out his hoofs to the heave of his flank,
And Charles, leaning forward, made certain, and cried,
"This is Cimmeroon's blood, blown in passing beside,
And Roy's going strangely was just that he felt
Death coming behind him, or blood that he smelt."

So Charles's heart lightened and Royal went steady
As a water bound seaward set free from an eddy,
As a water sucked downward to leap at a weir
Sucked swifter and swifter till it shoot like a spear.

There, a mile on ahead, was the Stand like a cliff,
Grey wood, packed with faces, under banners blown stiff,
Where, in two minutes more, they would cheer for him – if –
If he came to those horses still twelve lengths ahead.
"O Royal, you do it, or kill me!" he said.

They went at the hurdle as though it weren't there,
White splinters of hurdle flew up in the air,
And down, like a rabbit, went Syringa the mare;
Her man somersaulted right under Gavotte,
And Syringa went on but her rider did not.

But the little Gavotte tucked her feet away clear,
Just an inch to one side of the fallen man's ear,
With a flash of horse wisdom as she went on the wing,
Not to tread on man's body, that marvellous thing.

As in mill-streams in summer the dark water drifts
Petals mown in the hayfield skimmed over by swifts,
Petals blue from the speedwell or sweet from the lime,
And the fish rise to test them, as they float, for a time,
Yet they all loiter sluicewards and are whirled, and then drowned,
So the race swept the horses till they glimmered the ground.

Charles looked at those horses, and speedily guesst
That the roan horse, Red Ember, was one of the best;
He was level and easy, not turning a hair,
But with power all ready when his rider should care,
And he leaped like a lover and his coat still did shine.
Charles thought, "He's a wonder, and he's twelve lengths from mine."

There were others still in it, according to looks:
Sir Lopez, and Soyland, and Peterkinooks,
Counter Vair and Gavotte, all with plenty to spend;
Then Monkery worn, and The Ghost at his end.
But the roan horse, Red Ember, seemed playing a game.
Charles thought, "He's the winner; he can run us all tame."
The wind brought a tune and a faint noise of cheers,
Right Royal coquetted and cocked up his ears.

Charles saw his horse gaining; the going increased;
His touch on the mouth felt the soul of the beast,
And the heave of each muscle and the look of his eye
Said; "I'll come to those horses, and pass them, or die."

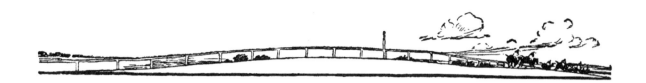

Like a thing in a dream the grey buildings drew nearer,
The babble rose louder and the organ's whine clearer,
The hurdle came closer, he rushed through its top
Like a comet in heaven that nothing can stop.

Then they strode the green grass for the Lost Lady's grave,
And Charles felt Right Royal rise up like a wave,
Like a wave far to seaward that lifts in a line
And advances to shoreward in a slipping incline,

And climbs, and comes toppling, and advances in glory,
Mounting inwards, marching onwards, with his shoulders all hoary,
Sweeping shorewards with a shouting to burst on the sand,
So Right Royal sent meaning through the rein in each hand.

Charles felt like a captain whose ship has long chased
Some ship better handled, better manned, better placed,
And has all day beheld her, that ship of his dream,
Bowing swanlike beyond him up a blue hill of gleam,
Yet, at dark, the wind rising makes his rival strike sail
While his own ship crowds canvas and comes within hail;

79

Till he see her, his rival, snouting into the grey,
Like a sea-rock in winter that stands and breaks spray,
And by lamplight goes past her in a roaring of song
Shouting, "Let fall your royals: stretch the halliards along!"

Now The Ghost dropped behind him, now his horses drew close.
Charles watched them, in praying, while his hopes rose and rose,
"O God, give me patience, give me luck, give me skill,
For he's going so grandly I think that he will."

They went at Lost Lady's like Severn at flood,
With an urging of horses and a squelching of mud;
By the hot flanks of horses the toppings were bruised,
And Syringa the manless swerved right and refused,

Swerved right on a sudden, as none could expect,
Straight into Right Royal, who slithered and pecked,
Though Charles held him up and got safely across,
He was round his nag's neck within touch of a toss.

He gat to his saddle, he never knew how;
What hope he had had was knocked out of him now,
But his courage came back as his terror declined,
He spoke to Right Royal and made up his mind.
He judged the lengths lost and the chance that remained,
And he followed his field, and he gained, and he gained.

He watched them, those horses, so splendid, so swift,
Whirled down the green roadway like leaves in the lift:
Now he measured their mettle, and said with a moan,
"They can beat me, Lord help me, though they give me a stone.
Red Ember's a wonder, and Soyland's the same,
And Gavotte there's a beauty, and she goes like a flame;
But Peterkinooks, that I used to despise,
Is the horse that must win if his looks are not lies."

Their bright colours flitted, as at dusk in Brazil
Bright birds reach the tree-tops when the land wind falls still,
When the sky is all scarlet on the tops of the treen
Comes a whirl of birds flying, blue and orange and green.

As a whirl of notes running in a fugue that men play,
And the thundering follows as the pipe flits away,
And the laughter comes after and the hautboys begin,
So they ran at the hurdle and scattered the whin.
As they leaped to the race-course the sun burst from cloud,
And like tumult in dream came the roar of the crowd.

For to right and to left, now, were crowded men yelling,
And a great cry boomed backward like muffled bells knelling,

And a surge of men running seemed to follow the race,
The horses all trembled and quickened their pace.

As the porpoise, grown weary of his rush through the dim
Of the unlitten silence where the swiftnesses swim,
Learns at sudden the tumult of a clipper bound home
And exults with this playmate and leaps in her foam,

Or as nightingales coming into England in May,
Coming songless at sunset, being worn with the way,
Settle spent in the twilight, drooping head under wing,
Yet are glad when the dark comes, while at moonrise they sing;

Or as fire on a hillside, by happy boys kindled,
That has burnt black a heath-tuft, scorcht a bramble, and dwindled,
Blown by wind yet arises in a wave of flogged flame,
So the souls of those horses to the testing time came.

Now they closed on their leaders, and the running increased,
They rushed down the arc curving round to the east;
All the air rang with roaring, all the peopled loud stands
Roared aloud from tense faces, shook with hats and waved hands.

So they cleared the green gorse-bush by bursting it through,
There was no time for thinking, there was scarce time to do.
Charles gritted his spirit as he charged through the gorse:
"You must just grin and suffer: sit still on your horse."

There in front was a hurdle and the Distance Post white,
And the long, green, broad Straight washed with wind and blown bright;

Now the roaring had screaming, bringing names to their ears:
"Come, Soyland!" "Sir Lopez!" Then cat-calls; then cheers.
"Sir Lopez! Sir Lopez!" then the jigging brass laughter
From the yellow tosst swing-boats swooping rafter to rafter.
Then the blare of all organs, then the roar of all throats,
And they shot past the side shows, the horses and boats.

Now the Wants of the Watchers whirled into the race
Like flames in their fury, like men in the face,
Mad-red from the Wanting that made them alive,
They fought with those horses or helped them to strive.

Like leaves blown on Hudson when maples turn gold,
They whirled in their colour, they clutched to catch hold,
They sang to the riders, they smote at their hearts
Like flakes of live fire; like castings of darts.

As a snow in Wisconsin when the darkness comes down,
Running white on the prairie, making all the air brown,
Blinding men with the hurry of its millions of feet,
So the Wants pelted on them, so they blinded and beat.

And like spirits calm shining upon horses of flame,
Came the Friends of those riders to shield them from shame,
White as fire white-burning, rushing each by his friend,
Singing songs of the glory of the world without end;

And as men in Wisconsin driving cars in the snow
Butt against its impulsion and face to the blow,
Tossing snow from their bonnets as a ship tosses foam,
So the Friends tossed the Wantings as they brought their friends home.

Now they charged the last hurdle that led to the Straight,
Charles longing to ride, though his spirit said "Wait."
He came to his horses as they came to the leap,
Eight hard-driven horses, eight men breathing deep.

On the left, as he leaped it, a flashing of brown
Kicking white on the grass, showed that Thankful was down;
Then a glance, right and left, showed that, barring all flukes,
It was Soyland's, Sir Lopez', or Peterkinooks'.

For Stormalong blundered and dwelt as he landed,
Counter Vair's man was beaten and Monkery stranded.
As he reached to Red Ember the man on the red
Cried, "Lord, Charlie Cothill, I thought you were dead!"

He passed the Red Ember, he came to the flank
Of Peterkinooks, whom he reached and then sank.
There were only two others, going level alone,
First the spotted cream jacket, then the blue, white and roan.

Up the street of green race-course they strained for the prize,
While the stands blurred with waving and the air shook with cries:
"Now, Sir Lopez!" "Come, Soyland!" "Now, Sir Lopez! Now, now!"
Then Charles judged his second, but he could not tell how.

But a glory of sureness leaped from horse into man,
And the man said, "Now, beauty," and the horse said, "I can."
And the long-weary Royal made an effort the more,
Though his heart thumped like drum-beats as he went to the fore.

Neck and neck went Sir Lopez and Soyland together,
Soyland first, a short head, with his neck all in lather;
Both were ridden their hardest, both were doing their best,
Right Royal reached Soyland and came to his chest.

There Soyland's man saw him with the heel of his eye,
A horse with an effort that could beat him or tie;
Then he glanced at Sir Lopez, and he bit through his lip,
And he drove in his spurs and he took up his whip.

There he lashed the game Soyland who had given his all,
And he gave three strides more, and then failed at the call,
And he dropped behind Royal like a leaf in a tide:
Then Sir Lopez and Royal ran on side by side.

There they looked at each other, and they rode, and were grim;
Charles thought, "That's Sir Lopez. I shall never beat him."
All the yells for Sir Lopez seemed to darken the air,
They were rushing past Emmy and the White Post was there.

He drew to Sir Lopez; but Sir Lopez drew clear;
Right Royal clung to him and crept to his ear.
Then the man on Sir Lopez judged the moment had come
For the last ounce of effort that would bring his horse home.

So he picked up his whip for three swift slashing blows,
And Sir Lopez drew clear, but Right Royal stuck close.
Charles sat still as stone, for he dared not to stir,
There was that in Right Royal that needed no spur.

In the trembling of an instant power leaped up within,
Royal's pride of high spirit not to let the bay win.
Up he went, past his withers, past his neck, to his head
With Sir Lopez' man lashing, Charles still, seeing red.

85

So they rushed for one second, then Sir Lopez shot out:
Charles thought, "There, he's done me, without any doubt.
Oh, come now, Right Royal!"
                              And Sir Lopez changed feet
And his ears went back level; Sir Lopez was beat.

Right Royal went past him, half an inch, half a head,
Half a neck, he was leading, for an instant he led;
Then a hooped black and coral flew up like a shot,
With a lightning-like effort from little Gavotte.

The little bright mare, made of nerves and steel springs,
Shot level beside him, shot ahead as with wings.
Charles felt his horse quicken, felt the desperate beat
Of the blood in his body from his knees to his feet.

Three terrible strides brought him up to the mare,
Then they rushed to wild shouting through a whirl of blown air;
Then Gavotte died to nothing; Soyland came once again
Till his muzzle just reached to the knot on his rein.

Then a whirl of urged horses thundered up, whipped and blown,
Soyland, Peterkinooks, and Red Ember the roan.
For an instant they challenged, then they drooped and were done;
Then the White Post shot backwards, Right Royal had won.

Won a half length from Soyland, Red Ember close third;
Fourth, Peterkinooks; fifth, Gavotte harshly spurred;
Sixth, Sir Lopez, whose rider said "Just at the Straight
He swerved at the hurdle and twisted a plate."

Then the numbers went up; then John Harding appeared
To lead in the Winner while the bookmakers cheered.
Then the riders weighed-in, and the meeting was over,
And bright Emmy Crowthorne could go with her lover.

For the bets on Right Royal which Cothill had made
The taker defaulted, they never were paid;
The taker went West, whence he sent Charles's bride
Silver bit-cups and headwork on antelope hide.

Charles married his lady, but he rode no more races;
He lives on the Downland on the blown grassy places,
Where he and Right Royal can canter for hours
On the flock-bitten turf full of tiny blue flowers.

There the Roman pitcht camp, there the Saxon kept sheep,
There he lives out this Living that no man can keep,
That is manful but a moment before it must pass,
Like the stars sweeping westward, like the wind on the grass.

THE END

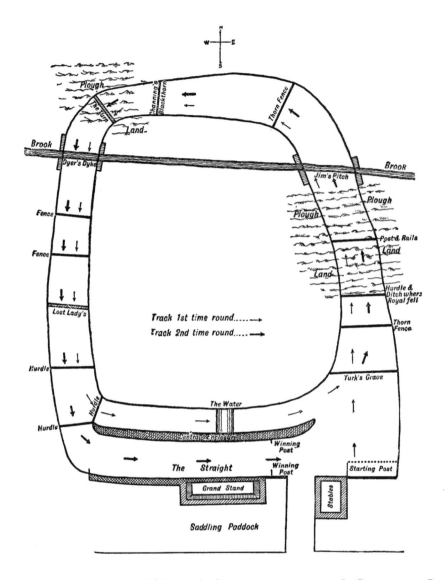

The course of the English 'Chasers' Cup is twice round Compton Course (about four and a half miles), over grass and ploughland with twenty-nine jumps.

Horses go round left-handed, counter-clockwise, from Starting Post, taking Turk's Grave fence as the first jump.

The first time round they do not enter the Straight, but keep to the left of the central enclosure and cross the water.

The second time round they enter the Straight, and finish just beyond the Grand Stand.

The circuit is two and a quarter miles.

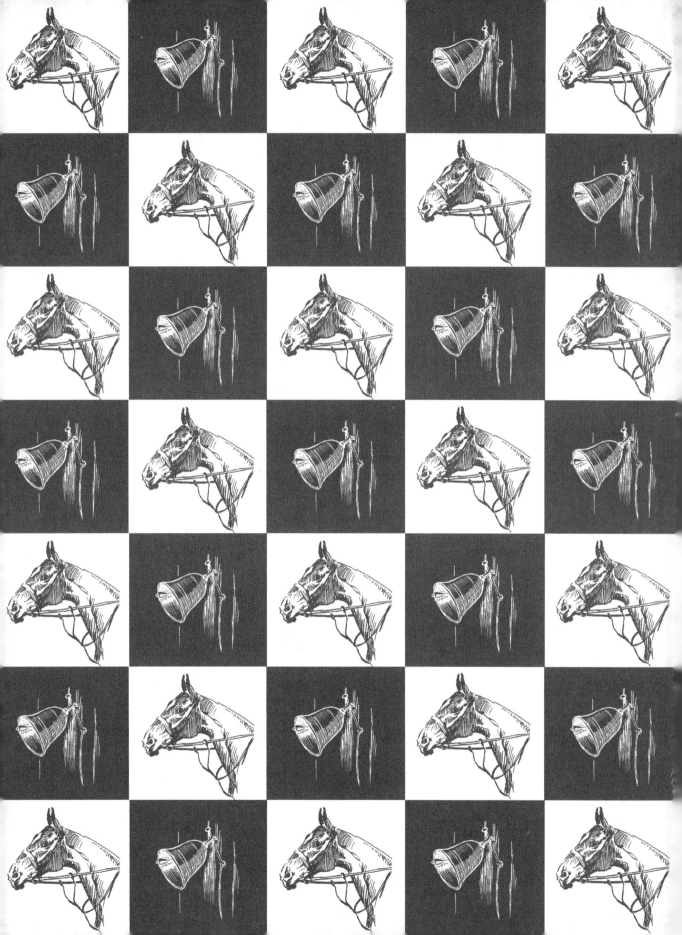